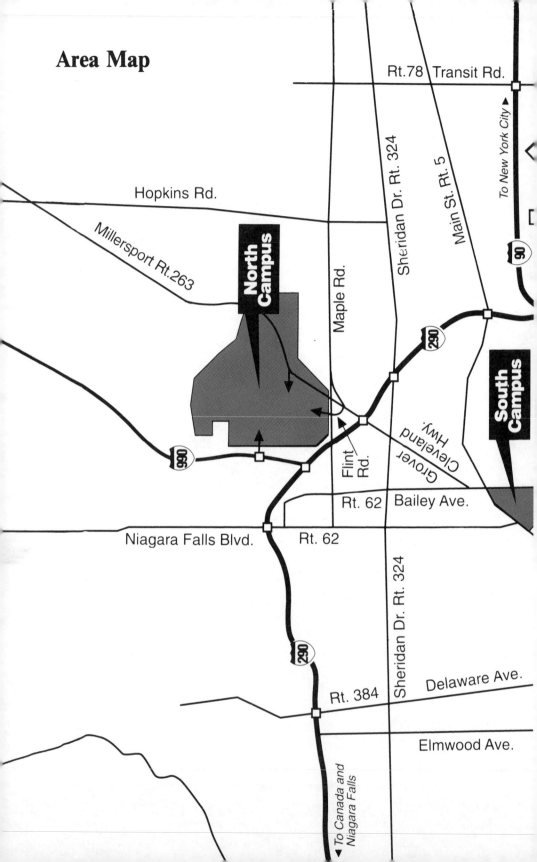

Area Map

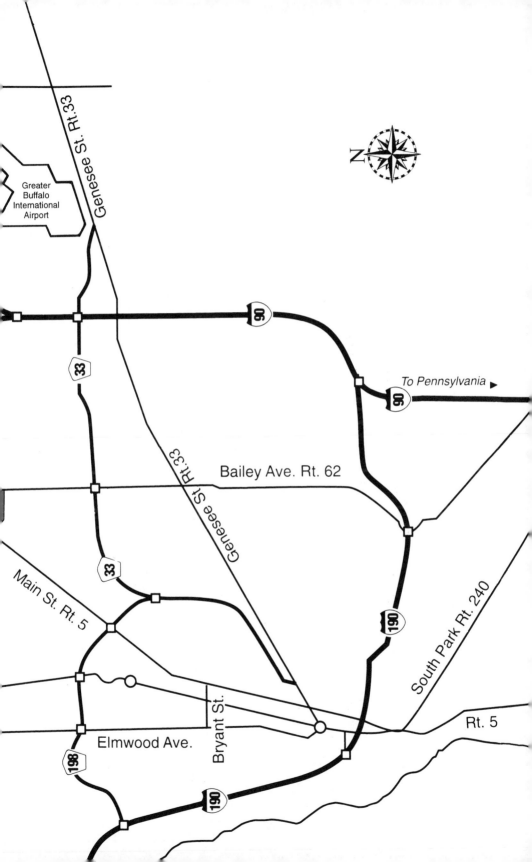

A Walking Tour of
The University at Buffalo

A Walking Tour of

The *University* at *Buffalo*

& Other Area Architectural Treasures
(Including a Driving Tour)

Frances Rupley

Prometheus Books • *Buffalo, New York*

Cover photographs
Front: Abbott Hall (former Lockwood Memorial Library—South Campus)
Back: Ellicott Complex (North Campus)

Published 1993 by Prometheus Books

97 96 95 94 93   5 4 3 2 1

Library of Congress Cataloging-in-Publication Data

Rupley, Frances.
    A walking tour of the University at Buffalo : and other area architectural
treasures / by Frances Rupley.
        p.   cm.
    Includes index.
    ISBN 0-87975-813-9 (alk. paper)
    1. State University of New York at Buffalo—Guidebooks. I. Title.
LD701.B43R87   1993
378.747'97—dc20   93-12107
                                                                    CIP

Printed in the United States of America on acid-free paper.

Contents

◆
_____

Acknowledgments

◆

Special thanks go to the following persons without whose assistance, support, and encouragement this guide would not have come about:

Robert Crowell reviewed with me the basics of writing a book.

Kate Payne suggested a tentative initial layout.

Harbans Grover and John Everett of the University Architect's Office and Jean Talcut of the University Publications Office provided campus building information and photographs.

Shonnie Finnegan and Chris Densmore of the University Archives provided much of the source material and historical photographs, and made valuable suggestions.

Catherine Linder spent many hours with me poring over archival photographs.

Jon Stauff assisted with the initial drafting of the building descriptions.

Professor Elizabeth Cromley read the text for architectural accuracy and provided valuable additions.

Annegret Richards walked the campuses with me to develop the walking tours, provided additional research material, made valuable suggestions, and assisted with proofreading.

Kay Lohnes and Louise Mink planned, developed, and mapped the driving tour.

Michael Sraga designed the maps for the walking tours.

Gwen Howard photographed many of the buildings.

George Rupley shot, developed, and printed many of the photographs of the buildings.

The Friends of the School of Architecture and Planning provided sponsorship, and Gerry Melton secured financing for the project.

My apologies to anyone I might have overlooked.

Dedication

Gerald Melton
1912–1992

Perseverance was Gerry's strength. He believed so strongly in the importance of this guidebook for the university, yet everywhere he turned for support he was met with resistance. However, he never gave up! When I remember Gerry it is with great respect and gratitude for his determination.

Glossary of Terms

Architrave. The lowest part of the entablature, the architrave sits directly upon the capital.

Art Deco. Part of the Modernistic style that was prevalent in the United States from 1920 to 1940, art deco is hallmarked by smooth walls with decorative geometric elements on the facade. A vertical emphasis is also present.

Ashlar masonry. Square-cut stones that are arranged in many different fashions (no course, irregular course, or regular course). Typical finishes for the surface of stones include natural or quarry face; sawed, tooled, or polished face finish.

Balustrade. A rail that includes an upper rail, balusters, and, occasionally, a bottom rail.

Buttresses. An exterior support of masonry that is attached to a wall.

Capital. The top part of a column. It may stand on its own or be surmounted by an entablature.

Cladding. Siding applied either vertically or horizontally to a building.

Column. A round shaft that acts as a structural support. It consists of a base, shaft, and capital.

Corinthian. The most elaborate of the columns as well as the thinnest, this employs two rows of decorative leaves on the capital and a highly decorated cornice. Most often associated with Roman architecture and ruins.

Cornice. Any molded projection that tops off a part to which it is joined. On a building, it is the exterior trim where roof and wall meet.

Doric. The sturdiest and least ornamental of the column groups, the Doric employs a simple capital, frieze, and a detailed cornice.

Elevation. The vertical face of a building or a drawing of the vertical face, either interior or exterior.

Entablature. That addition to a column that contains the architrave, frieze, and cornice.

Facing. A veneer of material used over a less attractive surface, e.g., plaster, metal.

Frieze. The middle section of an entablature, below the cornice and above the architrave. It can be plain or decorated.

Georgian. This prevailing style of eighteenth-century Britain and colonial Northern America shows the influence of Classical, Renaissance, and Baroque styles. Hallmarked by a decorative cornice, with windows and doors arranged in strict symmetry: often the door is surrounded by pilasters.

Gothic Revival. Popularized in the United States from 1840 to 1880 by the architectual pattern books of Andrew Jackson Davis and Andrew Jackson Downing, this style employs a steeply pitched roof and gables, decorative or "gingerbread" vergeboard, windows with a pointed arch, and a one-story porch that may be entry width or extend the full front length of the house.

Greek Revival. Popular in the United States from 1825 to 1860, this style emphasizes the use of Doric columns to support porches, elaborate details surrounding the doors, and a low-pitched roof, usually with a wide band of trim (imitating the classic entablature) emphasizing the cornice.

Ionic. Less solid and more ornate than the Doric column, the Ionian is hallmarked by a decorated capital, banded entablature, a continuous frieze, and a detailed cornice.

Mezzanine. A middle story, usually with a lower ceiling than the rest of the building stories.

Neoclassical. Popular in the United States from 1895 to 1950, neoclassical facades are dominated by symmetrically placed doors and windows and the presence of full-height porches supported by columns.

Pediment. The triangular gable end of a roof or a triangular or curved ornament used over doors or windows.

Pilaster. A pier or pillar that is attached to a wall and acts as a support. It may also appear as a purely decorative motif.

Portico. A porch that is supported by a row or rows of columns.

Prairie Style. Developed in Chicago at the turn of the twentieth century, the Prairie Style's most famous proponent was architect Frank Lloyd Wright. It is hallmarked by a low-pitched roof with wide, overhanging eaves; bands of windows, one-story porches, often with massive supports; and an emphasis on horizontal lines.

Romanesque (Richardson Romanesque). Patronized by American architect Henry Hobson Richardson, this style employs massive walls; large vaults; round arches over windows, porches, and doors; an asymmetrical facade; and towers that end in a cone-shaped roof.

Terra-Cotta. A very hard, unglazed, fired clay, used for ornamental and tile work.

Terrazzo. A mixture of marble and concrete that is ground smooth to utilize the marble sheen. It is used as a decorative surface for walls and floors.

Trusses. A triangular arrangement that creates a rigid support.

Tudor Style. A building style that was popular in the United States from 1890 to 1940. Hallmarked by steeply pitched roof; decorative half-timbering; tall, narrow windows arranged in groups; and massive chimneys.

Introduction

The University of Buffalo was incorporated by an act of the state legislature of New York in 1846. Although the impetus for this legislation lay in the need for a medical school to meet the health needs of a rapidly growing community, the charter also authorized academic, theological, and legal departments for this new institution. The School of Medicine was duly established and remained the only college until 1887. Millard Fillmore (president of the United States, 1850–1853) was named chancellor, an honorary and ceremonial position that he held until his death in 1874.

The medical school began its history in a leased building at Washington and Seneca Streets in Buffalo. In February 1847 seventy-two students received their first lectures from a faculty of seven physicians. In 1849 the university constructed its first building at Main and Virginia Streets. It was dedicated as the medical school, and it remained the only school in the university for forty years.

Expansion beyond the medical school came in the late 1880s and early 1900s, under the chancellorship of E. Carlton Sprague. Responding to demands of the city's pharmacists, the School of Pharmacy (the university's second division) was established in 1886. It was the first professional pharmaceutical facility in this part of the United States. A new building was designed on High Street in 1893 for the medical and pharmaceutical schools. A law school, established independently in 1887, was incorporated into the university in 1891, and in 1892 the School of Dentistry was added.

The twentieth century brought Charles P. Norton to the chancellorship. His leadership inspired the concept of "a greater university" that would include instruction in the liberal arts as well as undergraduate education in the existing professional schools. Courses in arts and sciences were set up in the High Street building and awarded departmental status in 1915. In 1916 a building on Niagara Square, owned by the Women's Educational and Industrial Union, became the home of the full-scale arts college, and in 1919 the State Department of Education authorized the College of Arts and Sciences to confer degrees.

In 1919 Walter P. Cooke, who became acting chancellor after Norton's retirement, initiated a citywide fundraising campaign for university development. In 1921, when the university observed its seventy-fifth anniversary and the arts college graduated its first class, an endowment was established and the necessary acreage acquired to consolidate its operations on one site.

By 1922, as the progress of the first two decades unfolded, it was clear that the university now required the leadership of an experienced educator to guide the institution into the future. Dr. Samuel P. Capen, a highly respected scholar, became the university's first full-time chancellor, a post he held for twenty-eight years, an era of innovation, growth, and change. This period of educational development was difficult from a financial point of view as the country moved ever closer toward the Great Depression and available resources were negligible.

Under Capen's direction, however, the achievement of quality was a major concern during this period between the two world wars. The loosely knit independent schools were woven into a coordinated system. More faculty were added and facilities and curriculums grew steadily. The College of Arts and Sciences was strengthened when graduate work and honors programs were introduced, giving the college a place within the university system equal to the professional schools. Its growth ultimately launched the schools of management, education, social work, and engineering. In addition, innovation and experimentation were also encouraged in the professions. Dental education became broader, a program in nursing was added to the School of Medicine, and scientific research expanded.

In 1946, as the university celebrated its centennial, a significant change was occurring on campus. The end of the Second World War and the subsequent G.I. Bill of Rights doubled the student population as the enrollment of veterans,

the nationwide economic boom, and the predicted population explosion in the 1960s and 1970s demanded the expansion of the university. A school of engineering opened in 1946, and the medical/dental complex moved into its quarters on campus in 1953. The evening division of the university and the last of the administrative offices followed, consolidating all the facilities, except the law school, on a central campus.

By the middle of this century, the University of Buffalo had become the largest institution of higher education in western New York State. Demands for educating an ever-increasing student population continued. From 1954 to 1963, Clifford C. Furnas, the university's ninth chancellor, guided the institution through an extensive program of curriculum enrichment and major building construction. The faculty grew; important scholarly resources were developed; university involvement in civic life, industrial growth, and the region's economic vigor expanded; and sponsored research expenditures spiralled. New buildings for professional departments and residence halls were constructed. The establishment of the first residence halls changed the role of the institution from a commuter college to a residential school and urban university.

In 1960 the state of New York moved to expand higher education opportunities. The opening of regional centers were considered, but mergers with existing institutions proved to be a financial advantage. In 1962 the University of Buffalo became the State University of New York at Buffalo (SUNY) and Chancellor Furnas its first president. As tuition and fees were substantially reduced in this public institution, applications for admission mushroomed. Construction moved slowly, renovations were made on existing buildings, and twelve temporary trailers and prefabricated facilities were erected for institutional use (some remain to this day). These space needs on the central campus, brought on by the merger, resulted in three considerations: expansion at the present site, relocation in Buffalo, or a move to one of the suburban areas. In 1964, with Nelson Rockefeller as governor, the announcement came from the state that the whole of SUNY/Buffalo would move to a new campus that would be developed three miles north of the present location, in the adjacent Town of Amherst. Ultimately, the decision was reached to convert the existing campus into a health sciences center.

In 1967 Martin Meyerson, formerly acting chancellor at the University of California at Berkeley, became president of SUNY/Buffalo. A man with a reputation for "frontier educational thinking," he challenged the university to adopt the "modern spirit" and to become a model for many. Under his leadership a series of plans for developing a number of separate colleges were introduced. At this point in the university's history, it should be mentioned that campuses across the country were in social and political turmoil because of the Vietnam War, and the University of Buffalo was no exception. Disruptive as numerous incidents were, there was a limited effect on the plans for the new campus.

In 1970 Robert Ketter, a member of the faculty and former Dean of the Graduate School and Vice-President for Facilities and Planning, assumed the presidency of the university, and construction on the new campus began in earnest. Adjustments were necessary due to runaway inflation, changing priorities, and an expected drop in the college-age population by the year 2000. Despite continued setbacks and delays, construction continued and by 1978 the North Campus, with approximately ten thousand students, became the official central campus; and South Campus was redesignated as the future Health Sciences Center.

In 1982 Steven B. Sample was inaugurated as the twelfth chief executive officer of the university, where he remained for ten years. The problems of dwindling resources and slow progress continued to plague the early years of his administration. Aware that uprooting the university had left its scars, he insisted that completion of facilities was paramount. In 1984 funds for final construction on both campuses were granted.

SUNY/Buffalo in the second half of the twentieth century has been embroiled in controversies, delays, restudies, and changes for almost thirty years, and the campuses are still under construction. It might appear that explosive growth created an almost new institution, but it is still a direct descendant of one of the first American universities based on the concept of providing for public need. Today, under its thirteenth chief executive officer, William R. Greiner, it continues to move ahead. There is a steady high enrollment and a wide range of academic and professional programs. It ranks among the leading public and private institutions in the quality of its graduate students, faculty, and programs, as well as the breadth and diversity and quality of its undergraduate programs in humanities, social sciences, natural sciences, and the fine arts.

South Campus

South Campus

Main Street Campus

Legend

1. Abbott Hall
   (Health Sciences Library)
2. Foster Hall
3. Crosby Hall
4. Hayes Hall
5. Wende Hall
6. Townsend Hall/Beck Hall
7. Parker Hall
8. Acheson Hall
9. Hayes D
10. Mackay Heating Plant
11. Clark Hall
12. Diefendorf Hall
13. Harriman Hall
14. Squire Hall
15. Cary-Farber-Sherman Halls
16. Dormitory Quadrangle
17. Goodyear Hall
18. Clement Hall
19. Allen Hall

X   Starting Point
● ● ●   Walking Tour

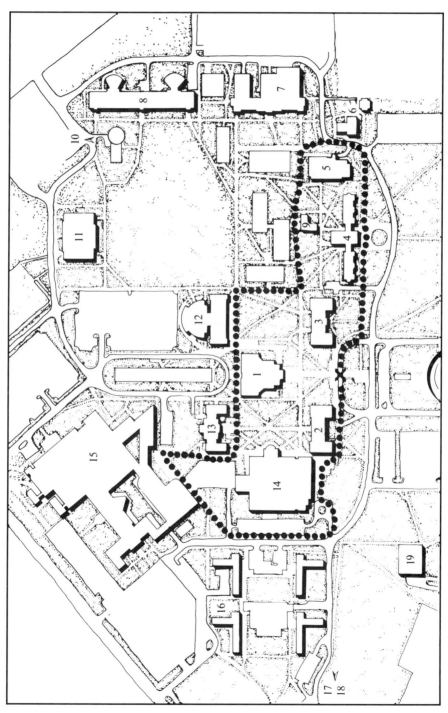

The walking tour, providing an over-view of the South Campus, takes about one hour.

In 1850, 154 acres of land were purchased by the county of Erie for an almshouse. The site was located on Main Street, outside the city limits, in the Buffalo Plains and along the Niagara Escarpment. From 1849 through 1903, buildings for an almshouse and an insane asylum were constructed, destroyed by fire, rebuilt in stone, and enlarged as the needs, facilities, and services expanded.

In 1908 the university purchased 106 acres of this land from the county, and by 1909 the deed to the land was transferred to the University of Buffalo. The First World War (1914–18) delayed the university's construction plans, but by 1919, a competition was announced for the design of the landscape for the future campus, and 44 adjoining acres were also purchased.

In 1920 the university council decided to build the campus in the classical colonial style and that native limestone should be used to blend in with the existing three-and-one-half story asylum that had been constructed in 1874. The New York City architectural firm of McKim, Mead, and White was selected.

In 1926 the entire asylum population on the site was transferred to new facilities in Alden (southeast of

Buffalo), and the university took control of the property. Renovations were made to the nurses' dormitory (Townsend); a third story added to the maternity ward (Wende); and the asylum (Hayes) acquired a neoclassical facade, a seven-hundred-seat auditorium, a new roof, and a clock/bell tower. A number of smaller buildings in the almshouse/asylum complex were removed.

During the 1930s, according to the design of E. B. Green, campus architects, the following buildings were erected: Beck, Crosby, Norton Union (Harriman), Lockwood Memorial Library (Abbott Hall), Clark Gym, and the Heating Plant (Mackay). This period of construction ends with the Parker Engineering Building (1946–49).

From 1909 to 1949, financial resources for building the South Campus came from private donors for a private university. Public monies were first used during the 1950s and 1960s, primarily for dormitories and classroom buildings.

In the 1980s, a $103.4 million project began. Foster Hall underwent complete rehabilitation to accommodate dental research. Additions were made to the medical school and the library, and Squire was converted to the dental school. The campus serves students, faculty, and staff in health science programs: medicine, dentistry, nursing, pharmacy, chemistry, and the health-related professions. The only academic units left on South Campus are the School of Architecture and Planning and the main offices of Millard Fillmore College, the evening school.

Two old stone buildings, Wende and Townsend, from 1885 and 1903 respectively, were slated for demolition, but they were saved when they were included as a subject of a studio project in the School of Architecture and Planning involving historic preservation and adaptive reuse.

It was during the 1930s that the important campus plan creating quadrangles for major campus construction was developed. This plan was prepared by Edward B. Green and Son and Albert Hart Hopkins, Buffalo architects, who had been charged by the university's Buildings and Grounds Committee to "investigate the whole matter of reconstruction of buildings and locations of buildings with a view of securing a harmonious treatment of all buildings and spaces involved."

Abbott Hall

Health Sciences Library

The library has played an extensive role in the life of the university since its dedication in 1935. Originally housing the collection of the Lockwood Memorial Library, the building, designed by E. B. Green and Son of Buffalo, has blended both old and new features, inside and out, to create a comfortable and graceful environment for study and research. After the relocation of Lockwood Library to the North Campus, the building was renamed, in 1977, after Charles D. Abbott, honoring the former director of university libraries. It is now conventionally referred to as Health Sciences Library (HSL).

Abbott Hall underwent an extensive renovation in the mid-1980s to serve the growing health sciences community more efficiently. It presently houses the Health Sciences Library and several functions of the Academic Services, Computing and Information Technology. It is considered one of the most modern medical libraries in the nation and is one of only nine medical libraries in the northeastern part of the United States.

Everyone involved in renovation was concerned with preserving as much of the old building as possible. An elegant building, modeled after the Villa Rotunda by the Renaissance architect Palladio, some consider it the best the university ever built. The present building, with its neoclassical facade and its modern research facilities, represents the university's reverence for the past while maintaining its commitment to the future.

The renovation architects, Scaffidi and Moore, seeking to preserve some historic characteristics of the building, maintained E. B. Green's design of the reading room featuring English oak paneling. The panels were carved by the Lipsett brothers, immigrants from Germany, who worked for Kittinger, a Buffalo furniture manufacturer. This old reading room was originally designed as a replica of a room built for the English Earls of Salisbury in the early seventeenth century. The room also includes a huge fireplace with a carved mantel duplicating one found in England's Canonbury Tower, dating from 1468.

The twin antique chandeliers, crafted in the 1840s, once graced the music room in the house of John J. Albright, a local philanthropist. His house was a large Tudor-style mansion also designed by E. B. Green. These silver-plated fixtures, originally designed for candles, were electrified when they were moved to the reading room in the 1930s.

Charles D. Abbott, a Rhodes scholar with degrees from Haverford, Columbia, and Oxford, was known both privately and professionally as a distinguished book collector. He founded the university's famous poetry collection, originating the plan for collecting poets' worksheets, manuscripts, letters, and first editions. He was also director of libraries from 1934 to 1960.

Foster Hall

Foster Hall was the first new building of the greater University of Buffalo Main Street Campus. It was designed by the New York City architectural firm of McKim, Mead, and White and dedicated in 1922.

The original structure was built of two types of Indiana limestone, gray and cream. In 1983 the building underwent extensive renovations under the direction of Buffalo architects Milstein, Wittek, and Davis. The original exterior details, such as the pediments and the similarity of the front and rear facades were maintained.

Foster Hall is used for nonclinical functions of the School of Dentistry. It contains student and faculty labs, offices, seminar rooms, and satellite animal laboratory facilities.

This building, originally the School of Pharmacy, was a $100,000 gift of Orrin Foster (1840–1928) and his family. Foster felt strongly that young people should take advantage of educational opportunities that he had never had.

Crosby Hall

Crosby Hall was designed by the firm of E. B. Green and Son, and opened in 1931. The exterior is faced with dark Queenston limestone, roughly finished. The trim, base, and entrance columns are a lighter, buff-colored Indiana limestone with a rubbed finish.

Notice the features of Crosby and Foster as to pediments, cornices, and pilasters. The two buildings make a nice pair both in color and in classical details. The rear elevation of Crosby is especially dynamic and "mannerist," full of violations of calm classical practice.

The balustrade running between Crosby and Foster Halls came from the residence of John J. Albright, where it had been for thirty years.

The building was originally occupied by the School of Business Administration and other departments over time. It presently houses studio space for the School of Architecture and Planning. The hall was named after the William Crosby family: William Crosby (d. 1944) was treasurer of the university.

Hayes Hall

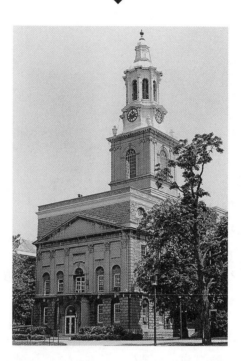

Hayes Hall, once part of the Erie County Almshouse and Poor Farm, was built in the mid–nineteenth century on 154 acres of farmland, safely away from the city center population. The first buildings were erected in 1849. Following several fires and epidemics, they were replaced with a stone almshouse in 1862 and a stone asylum in 1874. The architect for the latter was George Metzger of Buffalo. The 1874 construction and two later additions make up the shell of the present Hayes Hall.

The three-and-one-half story buildings of the Metzger almshouse/ asylum were built from limestone quarried on the grounds. The center of the facade of each wing had a hexagonal window bay providing the dayrooms with natural light and a panoramic view of the grounds. These wings were designed to separate female and male residents. The original stone buildings continued to function as the 100-bed county hospital for several decades.

In 1893 the inmates were moved to the new insane asylum on Forest Avenue, which is now the Buffalo Psychiatric Center. The university purchased the stone buildings and some additional acreage, and in 1926, under the direction of Jesse Porter of Buffalo, the complex underwent the transition from almshouse/asylum to the first phase of a university campus. The building was fitted with a neoclassical facade, a new roof and tower. In 1928 a clock, positioned 105 feet above ground, and a Westminster Chime, located 120 feet above ground, were installed in the tower. The Hayes Hall Clock Tower is one of the symbols of the university's philanthropic heritage and a neighborhood landmark.

The building was named for Brigadier General Edmund B. Hayes (1849–1923), a local engineer, businessman, bridge builder, and automobile manufacturer, who had bequeathed considerable funds for university development.

For many years Hayes Hall served as the university's administration headquarters. It presently houses the School of Architecture and Planning.

Wende Hall

Wende Hall, located south of Hayes Hall, was originally a maternity ward built in 1885 to serve residents of the almshouse/asylum complex. By 1888, the complex also included utility buildings (boiler, laundry, dining room, and kitchen). One of these stone structures, Hayes D, still stands. It was connected to Wende and Hayes Halls by a stone tunnel that supported an above-ground enclosed wooden corridor.

Early renovations were made by Buffalo architect Jesse Porter. Further renovations were completed in 1956 by Buffalo architects James, Meadows, and Howard.

When the complex first became university property, this building was renamed Hochstetter Hall. Ralph Hochstetter (1869–1955) was president of Cliff Petroleum Company and a director of Manufacturers Trust Company. His large bequests to the university made these renovations possible.

The building became the home of the Physics Department and contained the newest equipment and modern devices for research at that time. When the department moved to the North Campus in 1977, the building acquired the name of Grover William Wende (1866–1926), a graduate of the university medical school. It presently houses classrooms, offices of Academic Services, and the Media Study Department.

Townsend and Beck Halls

Townsend Hall

Townsend Hall (left), south of Wende Hall, and one of the older structures on the South Campus, was built originally as a nurses' dormitory for the Erie County Almshouse. It was designed by George Metzger and completed in 1903.

The structure was converted to educational purposes after purchase by the university, and it underwent extensive renovation directed by E. B. Green in 1931. Green removed the original porch on the side of the building and replaced it with a classical stone portico.

The building was named for Harriet Townsend, founder of the Women's Educational and Industrial Union in Buffalo. Plans for the future of Townsend Hall are undecided.

Beck Hall

When completed in 1931, Beck Hall (right) originally housed the university bookstore. The building, designed by E. B. Green of Buffalo, is modeled on the Holland Land Company building in nearby Batavia, New York. The Holland Land Company was the original developer of the city of Buffalo in the first decade of the nineteenth century.

This old building, at a time when the university was housed

mainly in downtown buildings, has served as a bookstore (1931–53) and a faculty club.

In 1977 the structure was renamed after George A. Beck, M.D. (1895–1975), a graduate of the medical school in 1919, who joined the faculty of the university in 1921. Beck Hall presently houses the Multidisciplinary Center on Aging.

Parker Hall

Parker Hall opened officially in 1946, the year of the university's centennial. The Buffalo architectural firm of Green, James, and Meadows designed the "E"-shaped building—three sections of equal capacity—for the new School of Engineering. When construction for the building was authorized, no one had foreseen the demand for engineering education and the huge increase in expected enrollment. In 1947 and 1948, two more units—T-shaped wings of two stories and basements—were added to the east and west ends of the building, providing additional laboratories, classrooms, and offices.

The building was named for Karr Parker (1893–1980), the president of Buffalo Electric Company from 1939 to 1977 and a member of the university council from 1945 to 1962. As chairman of the Buildings and Grounds Committee for fifteen years, he was responsible for completion of new facilities on the South Campus valued at $35 million, and was active in raising funds to establish the engineering school.

Acheson Hall

Chemistry became a popular major field of study in the early twentieth century when the university began training a high percentage of professional personnel. The State University of New York at Buffalo is located in an area with one of the world's largest concentrations of electro-chemical industries. To design a building that would provide students with an optimal education in the field, the university engaged the services of the architectural firm of Duane Lyman and Associates, of Buffalo, to design Acheson Hall, which was completed in 1959. It is a "nuts and bolts" building constructed with functionalism foremost in mind.

A large-capacity ventilation system, ample fume cupboards, easily accessible plumbing and wiring, large windows, and numerous exits serve the modern laboratory and classroom facilities in Acheson. The building was carefully planned with a view of incorporating all the latest features of modern design: no frills, but necessities that allowed the university to double the research and teaching activity of the Chemistry Department.

The chemistry building is named for Edward Goodrich Acheson (1856–1931), a self-made inventor/industrialist who had worked for Thomas Edison, developed silicon carbide, and founded the Carborundum Company in Niagara Falls. Within Acheson Hall, the George Barclay Bassett Auditorium honors the man who not only devised a simple and practical way to make water meters but founded the Buffalo Meter Company.

Hayes D

This old stone structure, made from limestone quarried on the site, was built in 1885. It is one of the remaining four buildings that comprised the original Erie County Almshouse/ Asylum.

Mackay Heating Plant

Originally the new central heating plant, this building, which was begun in 1931 and restored in 1973, is an architectural landmark as part of the master plan for the South Campus, prepared by E. B. Green. The ornamental chimney, with its Doric and Ionic columns at the top and enclosed in a stone tower, can be seen for miles around the campus and signals the university's presence to community residents.

In 1966 the building was re-named for Gerald F. Mackay (1906–1965) who joined the university staff in 1947 after many years as an industrial plant manager. Mackay was known as a man who was always motivated by a desire to render service to the academic program and do so at a minimum cost.

Clark Hall

Before the construction of Alumni Arena on the North Campus, Clark Hall housed the athletic program and recreational sports facilities for the university community. Built in 1938 and designed by E. B. Green and Son, Clark Hall is best known for its interior friezes of sport subjects. They are plaster casts of friezes made in Pelham, New York, for the 1928 Olympic Games. Students passing through the halls of the building have never been too far from these reminders of the classical beginnings of modern sport.

Clark Hall was named for Irwin Brayton Clark (d. 1924), a well-known Buffalo seed merchant.

Diefendorf Hall

Diefendorf Hall, one of the first structures to be opened after the merger between the University of Buffalo and the State University of New York, was designed by Duane Lyman and Associates and opened in 1963. Its modern design and use of concrete block, stone, and brick contrasts sharply with the stately buildings surrounding Hayes Hall.

The seal of the old University of Buffalo (in terrazzo) is featured on the floor of the central lobby.

This classroom building with three large semicircular lecture halls also houses the Mathematics Department. It is named after Charles Haas Diefendorf (1891–1975), a banker who was very active in civic, cultural, and philanthropic affairs in Buffalo.

Harriman Hall

E. B. Green and Son prepared the design for Harriman Hall on a prominent site opposite Foster Hall. Originally this structure was opened in 1934 under the name Norton Hall. The exterior of the building complements the neoclassical flavor of nearby Abbott Hall and the capitals and columns of Crosby and Foster halls, as well as the limestone of their construction. The building was modeled on the plan of a famous English home of Mershaw LeHatch in Kent, England, which was designed by the noted English architect Robert Adam.

The building was initially named for Charles P. Norton, who served as chancellor from 1905 to 1920. At a time when the university was entirely without endowment, he fathered the concept of the greater University of Buffalo by overseeing the purchase of 175 acres of land for what eventually became the South Campus on Main Street. Norton believed that it was very important for students to involve themselves in extracurricular activities, and for almost thirty years this building provided the facilities needed for student activities.

Norton bequeathed nearly his entire estate to the students of the university. In 1962, when a new student union was erected on the South Campus, the old Norton was renamed for Lewis G. Harriman (1890–1973), a businessman and civic leader in western New York and president of the Manufacturers and Traders Trust Company.

Squire Hall

Formerly named Charles P. Norton Hall, and then Norton Union, this building was dedicated in 1962. It served as a student center for twenty years. Designed by Duane Lyman and Associates, the building formed a rectangle with a second- and third-floor inner courtyard. Included were a concert hall, a movie theater, bowling alleys, and two large student lounges. Norton Union faced the dormitories on one side, and completed a quadrangle with classroom buildings and the library on the other side. It became a vibrant center for the varied facets of student life on campus, and it has been estimated that in its heyday about ten thousand people passed through Norton every day.

In 1978, as the university moved to the North Campus and the South Campus was designated to become the Health Sciences Center, the building was renamed Squire Hall for Dr. Daniel H. Squire (1869–1935), a graduate of the first dental school class in 1892. He also served as professor and dean of the dental school for twenty-five years. Plans for closing the union and commencing renovation became final in 1978 as well. This move left the students of the university without a student center. Very strong feelings about their loss emerged, and the furor that followed was reminiscent of the '60s.

In February 1982 Squire officially closed as a student union following years of protests, demonstrations, and, eventually, court cases, which spoke for the students' need for a sense of group identity with the university at large. A new student union opened on the North Campus in 1992.

Squire Hall reopened in 1986, renovated and enlarged by 80,000 square feet on the Main Street side, and became the site of the School of Dental Medicine. The firm of Rogers, Burgie, and Shahine of New York City were the architects. It houses four hundred dental chairs, student laboratories, and faculty and administrative offices. There is also a unique collection of old dental tools and dental equipment.

Cary–Farber–Sherman Halls

The schools of medicine and dentistry opened on the South Campus in 1953 and were originally named for Samuel P. Capen. Buffalo architects James and Meadows were charged with designing a building appropriate for the high standards of medical and dental schools in the nation, which would absorb the ever-changing developments occurring in the health sciences. This move of the school from downtown to a site on campus gave students the opportunity to make use of the new dormitories as well as the resources of the Arts and Sciences College. The building served one hundred medical and eighty dental students.

In 1987, under the direction of Cannon Design of Grand Island, New York, a $30 million addition was constructed. New exterior cladding was also added to the old buildings to bring them into harmony with the new construction. Another leap in the medical school's 140-year history, this addition enlarged its capacity by 35 percent.

Cary–Farber–Sherman houses one of the largest animal facilities in the United States, allowing activities of the basic science and clinical faculty to be better integrated, as well as more curriculum innovation and development. A new wing focuses on the quality of student life, providing a comfortable lobby, student organization offices, lockers, and lounges for faculty and staff.

Charles Cary was a graduate of the university, a member of the faculty for many years, a member of the university council, and former dean of the medical school (1882–

83). At his death in 1931 he left large financial bequests to the university.

Sidney Farber (1904–1973) graduated from the university and studied medicine at Harvard and in Germany. He was on the faculty of Harvard Medical School for forty-one years and became a specialist in leukemia and cancer in children.

DeWitt Halsey Sherman (1884–1976) studied medicine at the University of Pennsylvania and University of Buffalo. He became a professor of pediatrics in 1909, the first time pediatrics received recognition as a full-time specialty at the university's medical school. He also took an active role in the expansion of Children's Hospital in Buffalo.

Dormitory Quadrangle

The erection of Michael Hall in 1955 completed the east side of the quadrangle formed by McDonald, Schoellkopf, and Pritchard halls, which were constructed in 1953. These buildings are made of reinforced concrete frame with brick exterior, and facades, trim, and sills of limestone. They were designed by James and Meadows architects. The dormitories are built on a four-story "L"-shaped plan to house 450 students. Michael Hall is somewhat larger in order to house the university health services and clinic.

All four dormitories were locally financed, and they inaugurated a new era in the university's history. What had always been an essentially urban commuter university had now taken a first step toward becoming a residential university as well.

Edward Michael (1850–1951) was a member of the university council for half a century and chairman of the Buildings and Grounds Committee for thirty years. He was instrumental in the early design for the South Campus, the remodeling of many early buildings, and the construction of many new ones.

Lillias McDonald was the university's first dean of women and a strong advocate for student residences on campus.

Jacob Schoellkopf (d. 1942) developed the Hydro-Electric Authority at Niagara Falls and was instrumental in developing the area as a tourist attraction.

Mearl D. Pritchard (1900–1976) graduated from the School of Pharmacy in 1926 and was a well-known civic leader.

Goodyear Hall

James, Meadows, and Howard, a Buffalo architectural firm, designed the Ella Conger Goodyear Residence Hall. At its completion in 1960, it raised the university's residential capacity to 1500 students, a sign of continuing growth. At the time of its opening, university officials stated that, "Important as they are, beauty and decor are not the heart of Goodyear Hall. Individual rooms and facilities are more essential, and here, Goodyear is unique." The ten-story building features all the comforts of university residence hall life: telephones in every room, lounges on each floor, kitchenettes and laundry facilities, as well as various recreational facilities for students.

Ella Conger Goodyear (1853–1940), well-known for her philanthropy and her interest in the arts, was a strong supporter of the university. Among her many donations was a gift to the university libraries of a unique collection of correspondence and memorabilia of the famous actress, Katharine Cornell, who was raised in Buffalo.

Clement Hall

Clement Hall was designed by James, Meadows, and Howard and completed in 1964. The red brick dormitory consists of two lounges, recreation and study facilities, and rooms for five hundred students.

The building is named for Carolyn Tripp Clement (1861–1943), a distinguished community leader and philanthropist. Mrs. Clement gave twenty years of service to the University Council, taking particular interest in the buildings and grounds of the campus. She also endowed a Chair of Christian Methods at Yale School of Religion (Yale Divinity School). She donated her house at 786 Delaware Avenue to the Red Cross, and frequently made large financial gifts to the University of Buffalo.

Allen Hall

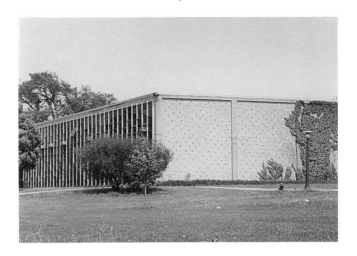

Originally Baird Hall, this concrete and smoked glass structure, situated on the northwestern portion of the South Campus, was built as the music portion of the proposed Fine Arts Center (which was never constructed on this campus). It was designed by Paul Schweiker of New Haven, Connecticut, and dedicated in 1957.

When the Music Department moved into a new Baird Hall on the North Campus in 1981, the former Baird Hall building was renamed in honor of Cornelia Hopkins Allen. As an associate professor of Social Work at the university, she supervised many programs between the School of Social Work and the community. After her retirement she became director of social services at Meyer Memorial Hospital (Erie County Medical Center) and became best known in the community for her work at Cradle Beach Camp, a facility for needy children in Angola, New York.

Allen Hall now serves as a facility for Alumni Relations and for WBFO-FM, the university's National Public Radio station.

This completes the walking tour of the South Campus.

North Campus

North Campus

Recent Buildings

A. UB Stadium   B. Natural Sciences and Mathematics

X   Starting Point
● ● ●   Walking Tour

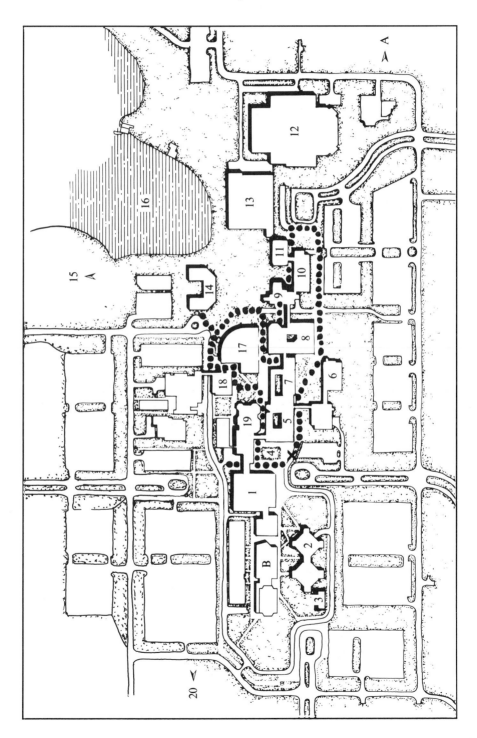

The walking tour of the North Campus takes about one hour.

Historically, the University of Buffalo, at the time of its incorporation into the State University of New York (SUNY), was a medium-sized institution responsible for the education of the children of the area's upwardly mobile middle class. However, the old, private, commuter-oriented school changed drastically following its absorption by Governor Nelson Rockefeller's massive state university system. In the years following the Second World War, economic, social, and political upheavals were occurring all over the country, and Buffalo was no exception to these pressures and demands for change.

The first change concerned the physical capacity of the university. A substantial increase in the student population, primarily resulting from the G.I. Bill of Rights, crowded the campus located on Main Street at the northeastern edge of the city. Enrollment had grown steadily since 1962, increasing the size and changing the face of the student population substantially. An ever-increasing number of students from other parts of New York State streamed into Buffalo, bringing with them a wide variety of social, political, and cultural backgrounds. Differences in ideas and points of view emerging from the university began to affect relations with the community. Issues of morality, censorship, freedom of choice, drugs, and music came to the fore, and an emergent anti-student stand became increasingly popular in western New York as well as in the rest of the nation.

Concurrently, in the mid-1960s, a master plan for an entirely new campus for SUNY/Buffalo was developed by the architectural firm of Sasaki, Dawson, and DeMay of Watertown, Massachusetts. It would be developed on a 1200-acre tract of marshland and marginal farmland seven times the size of the existing campus and at a projected cost of two-thirds of a billion dollars. At its conception, the master plan was visualized as the greatest architectural undertaking in American history; a boost to the economy of the Niagara Frontier; an addition to important engineering feats in the state of New York such as the Erie Canal, the State Thruway, and the St. Lawrence Seaway; and its electrical complex would be the largest in the world.

The central focus of the campus would be a grouping of buildings one thousand feet in width and one mile in length, from one to twelve stories high, whose designs would be assigned to nationally recognized architectural firms working in collaboration with Buffalo area firms. The projections for the 1980s were an enrollment of forty thousand students, which would attract the best teachers, researchers, and graduate students, and move the university into the upper ranks of public education.

Meanwhile, the university was still growing rapidly. On campus about twenty-five thousand students, faculty, and staff lived and worked in congested quarters as plans for the new suburban campus continued amid controversies over size, financing, and location. Land acquisition in the Town of Amherst continued as the clamor arose over alternate sites, such as a downtown waterfront location or the municipal golf course adjacent to the Main Street campus.

After months of wrangling and foot dragging, ground was broken on the Amherst site in October 1968, and a contract was awarded for the first building construction in June 1970 for the Governors Residence Halls (which, along with the law school, opened in Fall 1973). Construction continued through the 1970s, but as the university moved into the 1980s, plans fell on hard times. Projections for a forty-thousand-student body and a ten-thousand-member faculty had been in error. A declining pool of college-aged people, coupled with rising interest rates and state fiscal problems, eroded construction plans. When the North Campus is completed, it will have 60 percent of the original planned construction and 60 percent of the student population originally projected.

Despite building problems, SUNY/Buffalo has blossomed. The North Campus is unique in its central campus corridor, often referred to as the "spine." Offices, classrooms, recreational and lounge areas appear along the passageways that extend over roads and open areas to interconnect buildings. Inner courtyards, which are not visible from the streetside, break up the rush of academic traffic at the change of classes. There are libraries, study areas, and small resting places scattered here and there. In inclement weather, it is possible to walk inside interconnected buildings from Slee Hall to the east all the way to the western end of Talbert Hall, a distance of about one mile. In warmer weather, that same distance is punctuated with tables, benches, flowers, and shrubs along a series of outdoor plazas. Trees planted around buildings, along streets and walkways, are slowly reaching maturity, providing shade and slowing down the wind that often sweeps the campus. From a distance, the North Campus gives the appearance of a small city rising out of a plain, with its tall buildings silhouetted against the changing skies so characteristic of western New York.

Capen–Norton–Talbert Halls

Capen–Norton–Talbert halls are a series of linked buildings forming the westernmost end of the "spine." The firm of Sasaki, Dawson, and DeMay of Watertown, Massachusetts, served as the architects. This building, completed in 1977, is a focal point of student life and a meeting place for faculty and administration as well.

Capen has a wide base that steps back on the fifth floor, reflecting the differing functions of the lower floors where there is heavy traffic connected to the other spine buildings, and the self-containment of the upper administrative areas.

Capen houses the president's and other administrative offices and the University Libraries Administration, as well as the Undergraduate and Science and Engineering libraries, and the University Archives. The archives, with its ideal research facilities and comfortable reading lounge, provides a perfect retreat from the hectic pace elsewhere in the building.

Appropriately, this building was named after Samuel P. Capen (1878–1956), who, during his career as the university's first full-time chancellor (1922–50), molded a university out of a collection of scattered professional schools. Dr. Capen was a leader in American education policy as well as an important driving force behind the idea that students should study a broad array of arts and sciences, regardless of their fields of specialty.

The name Samuel P. Capen is remembered across the campus in a litany of tributes. Each year, Phi Beta Kappa awards a Capen Prize for the outstanding essay by a graduating senior; the Capen Award is the single most important award of the Alumni Association; the most prestigious chair in history is the Capen Professorship; and the first medical school on the South Campus was named in his honor. That distinction is now claimed by this multipurpose library/administration complex which stands at the center of the North Campus.

Talbert Hall honors Mary Burnett Talbert (1865–1923), one of the nation's most prominent black leaders, who came to Buffalo in 1894 and quickly became involved in the city's church and community life. Talbert was a writer and lecturer on social, political, and cultural issues; a civil and human rights activist and organizer; and a feminist and suffragette. Her efforts for African Americans led to the establishment of the National Association for Advancement of Colored People (NAACP).

Norton Hall was named after Charles P. Norton (1858–1923), a founder of the university's law school and the sixth chancellor (1909–1920). Norton fathered the concept of the greater University of Buffalo by overseeing the purchase of 175 acres of land for what eventually became the South Campus on Main Street. He also bequeathed almost his entire estate to the university for student activities.

Hochstetter–Cooke Halls

The original plans for the North Campus called for twenty identical linked towers to form the hub of the health sciences center to be located southwest of the "spine" buildings. In 1977 the university completed only two, both of which were designed by Hellmuth, Obata, and Kassabaum of St. Louis. Rising interest rates and declining enrollments necessitated a moratorium on new construction. The other eighteen towers were dropped when the university decided to renovate existing buildings on the South Campus and develop it as the Health Sciences Center.

At first glance, Hochstetter and Cooke Halls appear as tall as the ten-story Clemens Hall at the eastern end of the "spine." The towers, though, have only six stories. Above each story there is an interstitial space,

containing clear-spanning trusses and mechanical distributors, allowing for repair work and/or extensive renovation of the building for an alternative function without moving any walls or flooring. Each hall has a variety of instruction space on the ground floor, ranging from small classrooms to large lecture halls. Laboratory and faculty spaces take up most of the remaining stories.

One tower is named after Ralph Hochstetter (1870–1955), a native of Buffalo who had a successful career in banking and oil. Among his many philanthropic activities was a large bequest to the university for medical sciences research fellowships.

The other tower is named after Walter P. Cooke (1869–1931). A Buffalo attorney active in university life, Cooke recognized the university as the community's potentially most important institution. An expert fundraiser, he organized two important endowment drives in the 1920s, the first of which earned $5 million from twenty-four thousand subscribers. Cooke's mobilization of community support so impressed Samuel Capen that Capen accepted the position of chancellor of the University of Buffalo.

Dorsheimer Laboratory/Greenhouse

The one-story laboratory/greenhouse was designed by William L. Long Associates of Buffalo and completed in 1979. There are four separate greenhouse units, a total of 6,800 square feet, with environments ranging from tropical to "crisp." There is also a growth chamber and a botanical teaching laboratory.

Forty-five percent of the exterior shell consists of aluminum and glass, affording passersby a glimpse of colorful and bright plants on their way to classes; the remaining exterior wall is masonry with brick facing.

Students and faculty use the facility for instructional and research programs in biology and the botanical sciences.

Philip Dorsheimer (1797–1868) emigrated from Germany in 1816. He held several government posts under presidents Van Buren, Polk, and Lincoln, and also served as New York State Treasurer in 1859.

Founders Plaza

The Plaza, bounded by buildings housing the administration, some libraries, and the law school, serves as a central gathering place where students can congregate in pleasant weather. The grove of trees, plantings, paving, and benches provide surroundings where students are able to enjoy some sunshine, eat snacks, watch performers, and observe or participate in demonstrations.

Attached to Norton Hall and dedicated in 1988, the clock overlooking the plaza was donated by the graduating class of 1985. The students' dedication statement for their gift explained that "they owed something back in exchange for their educational development."

Founders Plaza is named in memory of all the individuals who were instrumental in establishing the university in 1846.

O'Brian Hall

After eighty-six years in downtown Buffalo locations and ten years of planning and preparation, the university's law school moved to its new quarters on the North Campus during the 1973–74 academic year. The building was designed by Harry Weese and Associates of Chicago and Anthony Carlino and Associates of Buffalo. O'Brian Hall was one of the first buildings to be occupied on the North Campus.

O'Brian is faced in "North Campus" brick. The south exterior is completely flat, but the buttresses on the north side serve the purpose of breaking up the monotony of the facade. O'Brian houses law and economics classrooms, faculty office space, law student advocacy groups, and the Charles B. Sears Law Library.

A distinctive architectural feature is the fifth-level open-air central courtyard surrounded on all four sides by the building's top two levels. The landscaped courtyard provides a relaxing area for a study break or a lunch hour in the fresh air or an opportunity to view changing art exhibits without leaving the premises. The seminar rooms on the top floors have large windows that provide magnificent views of the North Campus, particularly of the Lake LaSalle recreation area to the north.

The building is named for John Lord O'Brian (1874–1973). Buffalo-born, O'Brian graduated from the law school in 1893, served the nation in both world wars, practiced law in Washington, D.C., and held various government posts, including advising six presidents. Additionally, he served as National Chairman of Endowment of Harvard Divinity School, U.S. Attorney for western New York, and University Trustee from 1903 to 1929. He received the Chancellor's Award in 1940. O'Brian's life was one of eminent service to the city, state, and nation, and he was a man of high personal distinction who dignified Buffalo in the eyes of the world. O'Brian enjoyed the honor of learning, before he died, that the hall would bear his name.

Jacobs Management Center–Park Hall

The Jacobs–Park complex, designed by Hutchins, Evans, and Lefferts of New York City and Biggie-Schaflucas of Buffalo, is among the later additions to the North Campus, having been completed in 1986. The exterior of Park Hall is shaped like huge steps that descend to the south and west, prompting history teaching assistants to describe the buildings as "sawed off ziggurats." The design, however, provides maximum light and ventilation.

The red brick buildings, dotted by many small windows on each story, provide modern facilities for the School of Management and some social sciences departments. Jacobs Center has the offices of the business school's faculty, classroom space, and computer laboratory facilities. Park has limited classroom space but provides laboratory facilities, such as the Speech and Hearing Clinic and the Psychology Clinic, and seminar rooms. Park also provides long-awaited office space for the faculty of Social Sciences who, until this move, were scattered across the university. A glassed-in atrium serves as the entrance to the two-story building.

The Jacobs family of Delaware North Companies, whose name adorns the business school, is a leader in civic and philanthropic activity along the Niagara Frontier. Park Hall is named after Julian Park (1885–1965) who was the first dean of Arts and Sciences (1919–54) and served as the university's first historian. His father Dr. Roswell Park lends his name to the Roswell Park Memorial Institute, an internationally known facility in cancer research.

Baldy Hall

Baldy Hall is the home of Educational Studies, the Department of Philosophy, and the School of Information and Library Studies. It is another part of the "spine" designed by Harry Weese and Associates of Chicago and Anthony Carlino and Associates of Buffalo, and was completed in 1975. Upper level corridors flow physically and aesthetically from O'Brian Hall to Baldy Hall and to Lockwood Library. The corridor on the second level serves not only as circulation between buildings, but also as a snack/cafeteria area and provides a space for gathering, people-watching, and studying. There is also a two-level lobby and a circular conference room, the Kiva, which seats three hundred fifty people.

Baldy Hall's colorful interior artwork makes it one of the most visually inviting buildings on the North Campus. The wall murals were designed, sketched-out, and painted by students as part of a student design project that decorates three of Baldy's seven floors. The use of color and design were chosen by the students to complement the architectural characteristics of the "spine."

The opening of Baldy provided

Educational Studies relief from space shortages that had scattered two thousand students all over the university.

The building was named for Christopher Baldy (1885–1959), a Buffalo native who graduated from the law school in 1910. During a long and successful career, he was a member of the University Council from 1950 to 1959 and an active member of the Alumni Association. At his death he left a bequest of $1.5 million to the university.

Lockwood Memorial Library

Lockwood is a five-story, 230,000 square-foot steel-frame building of subdued red brick harmonizing with the warm tans to brown of the overall campus architecture. It was designed by the Chicago architectural firm of Harry Weese and Associates and Anthony Carlino of Buffalo. The Lockwood Memorial Library moved from its old home on the South Campus (Abbott Hall today) to the North Campus in 1978.

Lockwood Library has one of the finest collections of books, periodicals, and government documents in upstate New York. Essentially a six-story box, it utilizes various techniques in window design and indirect lighting to create a warm environment conducive to stress-free studying and research. This new version is a far cry from the stately style of its predecessor on the South Campus, famous for its majestic reading room and chandeliers. The beauty and formality of the former Lockwood that was abandoned for the raw practicality that encourages efficient use of space in circulation, cataloging, and photocopying may be justified in the incredibly important function the new Lockwood plays in the university community.

Reflective glass in Lockwood provides a view from inside affording privacy from without and minimizing heat and glare. An interior staircase spirals upward to a foyer leading to the circulation area. Outside, a steep staircase leads to a small garden. Study carrels and various reading areas are scattered around all floors, immediately adjacent to collections. A 1200 square-foot Friends Room with a two-sided woodburning fireplace dividing it acts as a social center and casual reading room for Friends of the Libraries, who maintain a recreational collection of twentieth-century literature and popular nonfiction.

Thomas B. Lockwood (1873–1947) was a Buffalo attorney who served on the University Council for twenty-eight years. The Lockwoods contributed $400,000 toward the original library, which was built in 1933.

Clemens Hall

One of the tallest buildings on either campus, Clemens Hall, designed by Ulrich Franzen and Associates of New York City, was completed in 1976. The Faculty of Arts and Letters administration and departments of English, Modern Languages, Classics, Art History, and others are found here. There are classrooms and offices for the university's renowned programs in Comparative Literature and American Studies. Language laboratory facilities are also available to help students complete the foreign language requirements of their general education studies.

The building is named for one of North America's most famous authors, Samuel Clemens (1855–1910), who, under the pseudonym Mark Twain, wrote the classics *Huckleberry Finn* and *Tom Sawyer.* Famous for his Mississippi River stories, Clemens made a mark on the Niagara Frontier when he moved to Buffalo in 1869 and became the editor and part-owner of the *Buffalo Express.*

Baird Music Hall

Student musicians, faculty, and visiting professionals have found a home in Baird Hall, designed by Ulrich Franzen and Associates and completed in 1981. The building houses classrooms, faculty studio-offices, a library, two multi-use rehearsal halls, and sixty-four student practice rooms. It also contains a modern recital hall, i.e., a multi-purpose performance room with three-part continuous seating and footlights, klieg lights, and a three-windowed control room. The insulated tinted windows and brown brick are designed to complement neighboring Clemens Hall, designed by the same architectural firm.

Baird Hall is named for the Baird family, which has played a very important role in the history of the University and the city of Buf-

falo. Frank Burkett Baird (1853–1939) came to Buffalo in 1888, built the Tonawanda Iron Company, developed the Hanna Furnace Company, and served on the board of the Pan American Exposition in 1901. He chaired the University of Buffalo Council and was a member of the Board of the University Foundation.

A philanthropist and an extremely successful industrialist who was a proponent of the construction of the Peace Bridge across the Niagara River to Canada, Frank Baird passed his fortune and his interest in the university to his sons Cameron (1905–1959) and William (1907–1987). Both sons carried on the family reputation in industry, founding the Buffalo Pipe and Foundry Company. An accomplished violinist with the Buffalo

Philharmonic Orchestra, Cameron's fondness for and skill in music led him to found the university's Department of Music in 1951. He held several executive posts with the Buffalo Philharmonic Orchestra and served as chair of the university's Department of Music until his death.

Slee Chamber Hall

Slee Hall, completed in 1981, is the last of the group of buildings designed by Ulrich Franzen and Associates in the late 1970s. It contains a 700-seat performance hall, two rehearsal rooms, a recording studio, an electronic music room, and support services for musicians, lighting crews, and sound personnel. It serves the university community as a showplace for major musical events and a hall for prominent guest artists and lecturers from all over the world.

Designed to conform to its neighbors, Slee shares the brown brick facades and tinted windows of Baird and Clemens Halls to which Slee is connected via a skyway. Inside, the hall features a magnificent self-contained, free-standing tracker action organ, custom made by C. B.

Fisk of Gloucester, Massachusetts. The organ has 1,826 pipes, 36 ranks, and 32 stops, and mechanical action between keys and pallet valves, admitting air under pressure to pipes.

The chamber hall is named after Frederick (1870–1954) and Alice Slee (1875–1956), Buffalo music aficionados who gave the university a $900,000 endowment to support annual performances of the entire cycle of Beethoven's string quartets. A professorship was also established to bring to the university's Department of Music composers of stature to give lectures, seminars, and concerts. Prominent composers including Virgil Thomson, Aaron Copland, and Lukas Foss have held the Slee Visiting Professorship.

Alumni Arena

The continuity of brown brick in the facade of Alumni Arena underlines a subtle attempt to integrate physical fitness and health awareness into the lives of the entire university community. The arena, a world-class sports facility that houses the university's NCAA Division I sports teams and faculty, was built in two phases (1982, 1985) according to the designs of Buffalo architect Robert Traynham Coles.

The cornerstone of the building is the main gym, known as the "A," featuring a hardwood floor the approximate size of a football field, a hanging curtain partition to maximize use of this open space, and a 288-by-264-foot roof in an innovative two-way pyramidal truss design. At full capacity, the "A" may seat about ten thousand spectators for basketball, wrestling, or volleyball. As the largest indoor gathering place, it is also used for guest lecturers and commencements.

The gem of phase two of Alumni Arena's construction is the natatorium, containing a fifty-meter Olympic pool with a separate diving well —accommodating everything from a one-meter springboard to a ten-meter platform. When filled to capacity, the pool holds 1.2 million gallons of water. Movable bulkheads also allow the creation of three pools. Due to the excellence of the natatorium, the university has hosted several NCAA swimming and diving championships as well as numerous state and local competitions.

Former president Steven Sample believed that a strong athletic program, if properly conducted by the university, would enrich and enhance the academic program. He hoped to engender a university spirit in the student body, alumni, and the business community—a spirit that had long suffered from the split campuses. He believed that creating a strong athletic program would lend a sense of student identification with the institution and lead to a stronger relationship between the university and the general public.

The athletic program moved from Division III to Division I level in 1991. In addition to competitive sports, the general university community makes constant use of the facility. Numerous racquetball and squash courts, an indoor running track atop the main gymnasium, auxiliary gymnasia, weight rooms, and generous locker facilities are open to students, faculty, staff, and alumni seven days a week.

The arena is dedicated to the alumni, the largest and most distinguished group in the university community.

Fine Arts Center

In the fall of 1989, the Fine Arts Center began taking shape along the shore of Lake LaSalle. When completed in 1993, enclosed corridors will link it to the adjacent Slee Hall and Alumni Arena. The New York City firm of Gwathmey, Siegel, and Associates developed the design with Buffalo architects Scaffidi and Moore.

The center is comprised of two buildings connected by an atrium with a continuous skylight. A standout on campus, inside and out, the exterior brick pattern forms horizontal stripes, and its whiteness is in sharp contrast to its neighbors. A covered entrance canopy extends from the two-story front of the atrium to Coventry Circle. A pedestrian plaza at the entrance to Slee Hall overlooks an enclosed paved area

for outdoor sculptures. The facade is similar in height to nearby Slee Hall and Alumni Arena, creating a sense of enclosure to the plaza. By contrast, the lake-side facade is at the bottom of a hill and two stories taller.

Inside the center are an 1800-seat theater with thrust and proscenium stage, a 360-seat drama theater with thrust and proscenium stage, a 200-seat experimental black box theater, a 150-seat experimental theater, a 200-seat media screening room, video production and sound studios, a general art gallery, a student art gallery, and two dance/performance studios. All major spaces are connected to the atrium, which serves as the center's main public entranceway.

The center invites all people in the community at large who are involved and interested in the arts. A recently formed arts advisory council promotes and supports artistic programs.

The Commons

Located on a thirteen-acre plot of land overlooking Lake LaSalle, the Commons is a commercial mall designed by Buffalo architect Charles Gordon to provide a modest range of shopping opportunities for people who live on, work on, and/or visit the North Campus. The Commons also offers employment opportunities for students. Built in 1990, it resembles a mini suburban shopping plaza and contrasts sharply with the urban look of the "spine." Its intent is to be a place where people can come together and be comfortable.

The site incorporates 50,000 square feet of stores, restaurants, recreation facilities, meeting rooms, and offices above the retail spaces, all clustered around a circular plaza. There is a courtyard and fountain surrounded by benches and spaces set aside for kiosks for student organizations and entrepreneurs.

Ellicott Complex

The Ellicott Complex, completed in 1974, is a thirty-eight building megastructure, basically consisting of dormitories, eating and drinking facilities, and administrative offices and classrooms. The complex was designed by the architectural firms of Davis, Brody, and Associates of New York City and Milstein, Wittek, Davis Associates of Buffalo.

Ellicott offers striking aesthetic aspects that combine both the height and the sprawl of the North Campus. The curving landforms and walkways heighten the visual appeal of the chunky forms and varying tower heights of the complex itself. By day, the eight-inch bricks, which are larger in surface than traditional bricks, display a range of warm tints that vary according to weather conditions. By night, the indirect light-ing along the window levels of the ground floor lends the buildings a look of weightlessness.

The principal aesthetic effect is best seen from a distance. When the sky is gray and low, one can see, from the highway, the contrast of reddish cubicle shapes, rising against the green flats, and, in the evening, the same shapes reflecting across Lake LaSalle.

The original conception for Ellicott was to create the ultimate work of academic integration in the complex, i.e., a set of buildings combining the heavy human traffic of a university with the ample green space of the surrounding environment; a peaceful and constructive coexistence of academic, administrative, extra-curricular, cultural, and student/faculty living spaces; a multi-purpose structure built to reflect both natural and climatic changes and the oscillating moods of members of the university community.

Ellicott offers an extraordinary range of options for moving from one point to another. The buildings are planned around courtyards, visible through extensive windows. There are also indoor/outdoor routes along the core and numerous combinations of both. The interior passageways are dotted with large window-walls, providing visual interaction with the landscape, particularly the large grove of trees that was preserved during construction. The confusions experienced by those who have used the buildings have become proverbial.

Ellicott was intended to house thirty-two hundred resident students in dormitories and to supply an additional twenty-seven hundred commuters with classrooms, libraries, a bookstore, a club, eating facilities, a health services center, lounges, and numerous other support services. The complex was to be divided into six colleges in the way of the English university system, in which students with an interest in ecology, mathematics, humanities, and the arts could live together in a homogeneous learning situation. The colleges radiated from an L-shaped core, an "avenue of scholastic activities" that incorporates a bus tunnel, two libraries, a bookstore, classrooms, faculty offices, food services, a theater, and an auditorium.

The college system has been almost entirely dismantled in subsequent years, and most of Ellicott's buildings now serve as dormitories. The complex still houses the Katharine Cornell Theatre, named for the famous Buffalo actress and supporter of the performing arts in Western New York. She received the Chancellor's Award in 1935. The theater hosts a variety of events throughout the year, including the coast-to-coast televised broadcasts of the political satirist Mark Russell, a former Buffalonian.

Joseph Ellicott (1760–1826) was the first resident agent of the Holland Land Company who surveyed the Western New York wilderness in 1798. An early advocate of the Erie Canal, he also mapped out a radial-on-grid plan for the city of Buffalo, similar in design to the earlier plan for Washington, D.C.

Lake LaSalle and Baird Point

A focal point of the North Campus, the lake covers sixty acres, has two miles of shoreline, and has average and maximum depths of ten feet and twenty-five feet. Designed by the creators of the university's master plan, Sasaki, Dawson, and DeMay, its purpose was to provide flood control and storm water runoff from a swampy site and to be used for future educational and recreational use.

In 1959, when the old Federal Reserve Bank in downtown Buffalo was faced with demolition, a proposal was made to save and move the Greek Ionic columns to the university as a memorial to servicewomen and -men. Each column has five sections plus a base. They now stand on Baird Point, overlooking the lake, in a setting designed by Buffalo architect Peter Castle.

The lake was named after the famous French explorer LaSalle who sailed the first European ship into what is now the Buffalo Harbor in 1678.

Student Union

The Student Union, which opened in 1992, was designed by Stieglitz, Stieglitz, and Tries. The 75,000 square-foot building features a theater, food facilities, recreation center, music room, multi-purpose conference center with a capacity for four hundred people, and movable walls and partitions. It offers a central location for the ninety to one hundred student organizations that had been spread all over the campuses.

A student union is the center of student life, a central core campus activity that contributes to the quality of life beyond the classroom. After the closing of Norton Union on South Campus in 1982, the students began congregating in Capen Lobby, revealing their longing for a community identity with the university. After ten years without a legitimate meeting and gathering place, the opening of the student union in 1992 was a vital part of the effort to make the university a complete campus. (See also Squire Hall on South Campus.)

Engineering Quadrangle
(Bell, Furnas, Jarvis, Ketter Halls)

The engineering and applied sciences cluster, erected during the period 1973–81, provides the university's highly rated engineering departments with excellent research and teaching facilities. The buildings are a departure from the *de rigeur* brown brick surfaces of the North Campus. The design of Marcel Breuer and Associates of New York City, in conjunction with Cannon Design of Grand Island, New York, features charcoal-colored brick-faced structures with precast concrete trim that creates a unique identity for the quadrangle. The highly specialized nature of the various curricula required a variety of engineering facilities, including the Earthquake Center.

Bell Hall, a three-story structure, was completed in 1975. It houses the Department of Industrial Engineering and contains special engineering research offices where individual projects are conducted, as well as space for man-machine systems and human factors research for designing tools, objects, and working environments suitable for human labor.

The building is named after Lawrence D. Bell (1894–1956), an experimenter and local leader in the field of aviation. He was the founder of Bell Aerosystems and the developer of the Bell helicopter. The Bell Foundation provides an endowed chair in his name in the Department of Philosophy and a general purpose fund in the School of Engineering.

Furnas Hall is a ten-level structure completed in 1977. It houses the Departments of Chemical and

Mechanical Engineering and provides space for systems design research and an interaction computation laboratory with process computers.

The building was named after Clifford C. Furnas (1900–1969), a primary force in the negotiations and decision to merge the private University of Buffalo with the State University of New York. Under his direction as chancellor (1954–62) and subsequently as president of SUNY at Buffalo (1962–66), twenty-two new buildings were erected, the faculty doubled in size from twelve hundred to twenty-four hundred, research funds increased substantially, and the University of Buffalo Foundation was established.

Jarvis Hall, the mechanical and electrical engineering sciences building, was completed in 1981. It was named after Gregory B. Jarvis (1944–86), a 1967 graduate of the university's electrical engineering program who, with six others, lost his life on the space shuttle *Challenger* explosion in 1986. An inspiration to students, Jarvis gave the commencement address to engineering and applied science students in 1985.

After Jarvis's death, students nailed a sign reading "Jarvis Hall" to the building in his honor. The name was made official in a 1987 dedication ceremony. A university flag recovered from the *Challenger* wreckage and a bronze bust of Jarvis, a gift from the senior class of 1987, are in the University Archives.

Ketter Hall, the civil engineering building completed in 1981, is also the site of the $1.5 million earthquake simulator, one of only five in the world and considered the most versatile in North America.

The building is named after Robert L. Ketter (1928–89), a professor of Civil Engineering who served as graduate school dean (1965–67), facilities planning dean (1967–70), and president of the university (1970–82). During his tenure, he not only strengthened the university's reputation for educational excellence, but additionally planned and implemented one of the largest building programs undertaken by any educational institution in the nation. Returning to teaching after his tenure as president, Ketter participated in the university's successful bid to host the National Center for Earthquake Research.

Knox Lecture Hall

Knox Hall was designed by the Buffalo firm of Hamilton, Houston, and Lownie. When the building opened in 1981, Knox supplied enough classroom space to curtail somewhat the endless shuttling of students and faculty between the two campuses. This building presents an impressive main entrance with a skylight and staircase, spacious lounges on two floors, one large hall accommodating four hundred fifty students, three medium-sized halls for two hundred fifty students each; and two smaller classrooms for ninety students each.

The outstanding lecture facilities include projection booths, retractable screens, and fully equipped demonstration benches for wet lab experiments.

The building is named for Grace Knox (1862–1936), who generously provided the university with the means to establish the College of Arts and Sciences after the death of her husband, Seymour Knox. The Knox family continues to serve both the university and the greater Buffalo area as civic, cultural, and philanthropic leaders.

Governors Residence Halls

These dormitories, completed in 1975 and honoring four New York State governors, were designed by I. M. Pei of New York City. The plan is a replica of the Pei dormitory design for SUNY/Fredonia (sixty-five miles southwest of Buffalo), containing spaces for over eight hundred resident students in four-bedroom suites.

The complex has been said to embody a "medieval-modern" style, emphasizing a fortress-like solidity in appearance. The first story is devoted to wide sweeps of lounges with glass and white concrete. The two upper stories of red brick enclose the students' rooms. Dining facilities are arranged as a group of cafe-like eating spaces, and patios and balconies are distributed about the structure.

Each building is an "H" in plan. The insides of each "H" form a small courtyard with two paved brick pathways intersecting at right angles and bordered by brick walls to enclose the yards. The four "Hs" form a large central courtyard designed for large congregations of students. The open spaces surrounding the complex encourage pickup games of softball and frisbee in pleasant weather.

The Governors honored are:

DeWitt Clinton (1769–1828)— Four times governor of New York. The Erie Canal was built during his term of office.

Theodore Roosevelt (1858–1919)—governor 1898–1900, president of the United States 1901–1909.

Herbert Lehman (1878–1963)— governor 1933–42.

Thomas E. Dewey (1903–1971)—governor 1943–54.

This concludes the walking tour of the North Campus.

Driving Tour

Driving Tour

Legend

1. Darwin D. Martin House
2. Gardener's Cottage
3. George Barton House
4. Delaware Park
5. Buffalo and Erie County Historical Society
6. Albright-Knox Art Gallery
7. Rockwell Hall
8. Buffalo Psychiatric Center
9. 800 West Ferry Street
10. Williams-Butler House
11. Mayfair Lane
12. Kleinhans Music Hall
13. First Presbyterian Church
14. Arlington Park
15. City Hall
16. Old County Hall
17. Guaranty Building
18. St. Paul's Episcopal Cathedral
19. Ellicott Square Building
20. Erie Community College City Campus
21. Dun Building
22. Pilot Field
23. Buffalo Skyline
24. Buffalo Waterfront
25. Illuminating Gas Company
26. The Midway
27. Wilcox House
28. Forest Lawn Cemetery

N

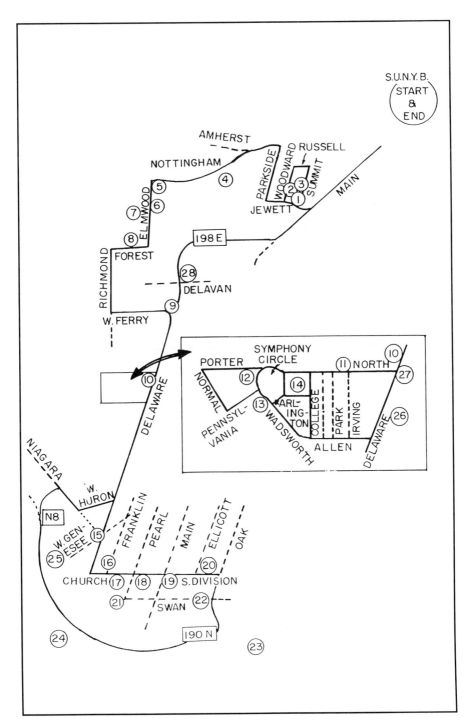

This tour can take one-and-a-half to three hours to drive, and it has several sites at which you might wish to park and walk. NOTE: Some buildings are privately owned and are not open to the public.

When Joseph Ellicott first laid out the street plan for the city of Buffalo in 1797, he planned a plaza with radiating main streets over a series of grids of smaller streets where Niagara Square now stands. In 1868 Frederick Law Olmsted joined together much of the growing city with a series of green parks.

At the turn of this century, Buffalo was one of the largest and most prosperous cities in the United States. It had a rich cultural and religious diversity, attracting immigrants from all of Europe to its many industries and transportation centers. These groups then formed ethnic neighborhoods, many of which remain. Buf-

falo was also a stop on the Underground Railroad for escaped slaves from the South on their way to Canada. Many African-Americans moved from southern states to Buffalo for the defense work available here during World War II.

This tour will take you downtown through some of the neighborhoods and past some of the buildings that make Buffalo famous for its architectural heritage.

Starting at the South Campus of the University at Buffalo, drive south on Main Street for about 1.8 miles and turn right on Jewett Parkway. You will now see three Frank Lloyd Wright houses. After passing the first of these at 125 Jewett Parkway, turn right on Woodward Avenue, right on Russell Avenue, turn right on Summit Avenue, and right again on Jewett. Circling this block takes you past the three Wright houses.

Darwin D. Martin House

125 Jewett Parkway

This famous "Prairie House" is characterized by strong horizontal lines, as seen in its chimneys, low roof, wide overhangs, and bands of windows. The interior features rooms that flow together in an open floor plan; ceilings of varying heights and shapes; natural materials of brick, oak, and plaster; warm earth tones, and indirect lighting. Many of the original art glass windows and furnishings designed by Wright are still intact. The design was revolutionary and cost about $100,000 to build. Originally the complex of three houses also included a long covered walkway (pergola) that connected the main house to a conservatory, with a two-story garage, stables, and chauffeur's apartment to the left. These structures were demolished by a subsequent owner, as was much of the landscaping that made the house appear to be part of nature.

Darwin D. Martin was director of the Larkin Company, a large local soap and mail order business. Wright also designed the innovative Larkin administration building (demolished in 1950), and an additional two residences for officers of the Larkin Company, for a total of five Prairie Houses in Buffalo.

This national historic landmark is owned by the University at Buffalo. A joint university, state, and private management group has begun fund-raising for restoration and eventual reopening.

1905 Architect: Frank Lloyd Wright

Gardener's Cottage

285 Woodward Avenue

This small frame and stucco house with art glass windows was designed for the gardener of the extensive grounds of the Martin complex. It has recently been restored and has a new addition in back that is sympathetic to the original design. The exterior colors are supposedly close to the original earth tones.

1905 Architect: Frank Lloyd Wright

George Barton House

118 Summit Avenue

Designed for Darwin D. Martin's sister, Delta, and her husband George Barton, this was the first house to be completed in the Martin complex, which included the site where the three apartment buildings now stand. Although the rooms are smaller than those in the Martin house, the central living spaces are also open to each other. The house also follows a cross-axial plan and has a low profile that makes it appear secured to the earth. It, too, emphasizes straight lines and right angles, and features art glass windows. It is interesting to see these three Wright houses in contrast to the neighboring ones built from the 1880s to the 1920s.

1904 Architect: Frank Lloyd Wright

Proceed to the end of Jewett Parkway, turn right on Parkside Avenue, left on Amherst Street, left on Nottingham Terrace, and cross Delaware Avenue to a left on Elmwood Avenue.

Delaware Park

This area was planned as a part of a major park system connecting all of Buffalo's neighborhoods. Since 1870 it has been in continuous use. Its open spaces, curving drives, and small ornamental lakes became Olmsted trademarks in his parks throughout the United States. The parkways of Buffalo connected a series of parks and helped to create planned neighborhoods. You will pass the Buffalo Zoo and many other recreational facilities contained in this park. The Pan-American Exposition of 1901 was situated at the northwest edge of the park, near the next viewing site.

1870 Designer: Frederick Law
                 Olmsted

Buffalo and Erie County Historical Society

25 Nottingham Court

Overlooking the Delaware Park lake, this handsome neoclassical building of Vermont marble was built for the Pan-American Exposition of 1901 as the New York State Pavilion, and was the only permanent building at the exposition. Wings were added in 1925. The museum has many interesting exhibits relating to Buffalo and Erie County history.

The building is a national historic landmark.

1901 Architect: George Cary

Drive south on Elmwood Avenue. The Gallery is on the left, the College on the right.

Albright-Knox Art Gallery

1285 Elmwood Avenue

The art gallery was built for John J. Albright, a wealthy Buffalo industrialist, as his gift to the people of Buffalo. It was built in the neoclassical style of a Greek temple. In 1933, Seymour Knox, art patron and financier, became a great supporter. The gallery is world renowned as a center for modern art. In 1962, a marble and glass wing was added.

1905 Architects: Green and Wicks
1962 Architects: Gordon Bunshaft of Skidmore, Owings, and Merrill

Rockwell Hall

1300 Elmwood Avenue

7

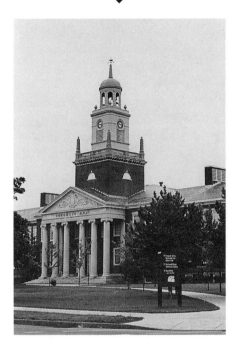

This colonial style building is the administrative center for Buffalo State College. It contains the Burchfield Art Center, which has a large collection of paintings by the Buffalo artist Charles Burchfield, and continuously changing shows of Western New York artists. Two rooms from the Metcalfe House (1884) have been restored and are on display here. (See note on the Williams–Butler House.)

1928 Architect: William Haugaard

Turn right on Forest Avenue. Buffalo Psychiatric Center will be on the right.

Buffalo Psychiatric Center

400 Forest Avenue at Elmwood Avenue

This asylum was built as a series of connected pavilions, each meant to house a different category of patient. Constructed of Medina sandstone and brick, Richardson's design for the building was his personal revival of the Romanesque style, and was considered innovative. It was visited by many international health professionals. The grounds were designed by Frederick Law Olmsted, the great landscape architect, and included parks and productive farms worked by the patients. Most of this farmland is now occupied by the campus of the State University College at Buffalo.

The building is designated a national historic landmark.

1870–96 Architect: H. H. Richardson

Turn left on Richmond Avenue around Colonial Circle. Stay on Richmond, then turn left on West Ferry Street to Delaware Avenue.

800 West Ferry Street

at Delaware Avenue

This ten-story building, which popularized luxury apartment living in Buffalo in the early twentieth century, was built for Darwin R. Martin, son of Darwin D. Martin who built the largest Frank Lloyd Wright house in Buffalo.

Typical of these apartments are two-level units, fireplaces, and beamed ceilings. An unusual feature at the time was the incorporation of large terraces reminiscent of single residences gathered into a high-rise structure. Presently, many of the spacious apartments have been modified to small condominium layouts.

1929 Architects: Bley and Lyman

Turn right on Delaware Avenue and proceed south.

Williams–Butler House

Delaware Avenue at North Street

This structure was built as a stately mansion at a cost of $175,000 and was considered to be one of the finest houses in Buffalo. The splendid Corinthian portico leads into a broad central hall with an open staircase and a chandelier hung from the upper floor. It was built by the banker George Williams, and later occupied by Edward Butler, the publisher of the *Evening News.* The brother of George Williams built a smaller but equally impressive house next door at 690 Delaware, known as the Williams–Pratt House. Both of these houses once had elaborate gardens.

The Williams–Butler House was restored by Delaware North Companies, Inc., under an agreement that allowed the Metcalfe House at 125 North Street to be demolished in 1980. The paneled hall and staircase of the Metcalfe House went to the Metropolitan Museum of Art in New York City, where they were restored and opened as a permanent exhibit in December 1991. The dining room and library were restored and installed in Rockwell Hall at the State University College at Buffalo, where they may be viewed by appointment. Subsequent restoration has been undertaken by the current owner, the Verity Corporation.

1898 Architects: McKim, Mead, and White

Turn right on North Street. To view Mayfair Lane, stop and walk up the stairs (opposite Irving Street).

Mayfair Lane

North Street on right between Irving and Park Streets

This design recreates an English village in a contained city environment. Using stucco, wood, and bricks over steel and concrete, the "village" is composed of twenty town houses facing each other over a broad walkway, with a small manor house at the end once occupied by E. B. Green, Jr. Garages and servant quarters were placed under this raised village. For a closer look at this charming complex, you have to park and walk up.

1928 Architects: E. B. Green and Son and Hopkins

Proceed on North Street to Symphony Circle, turn left on the Circle and right on Pennsylvania Street, right on Normal Street, right on Porter Avenue, and right again on Symphony Circle to an immediate left on Wadsworth Street. This will take you around Kleinhans Music Hall and past the First Presbyterian Church.

Kleinhans Music Hall

Symphony Circle

This celebrated concert hall is renowned for its acoustical excellence and is the home of the Buffalo Philharmonic Orchestra. It was an early collaboration of Eliel Saarinen and his son Eero, and is still considered one of the most successful concert halls in the United States. Its curved exterior and clean lines are repeated in the interior with wide, open stairways and a mezzanine leading into a paneled auditorium.

The building is designated a national historic landmark.

1940 Architects: Eliel and Eero
                   Saarinen

First Presbyterian Church

1 Symphony Circle

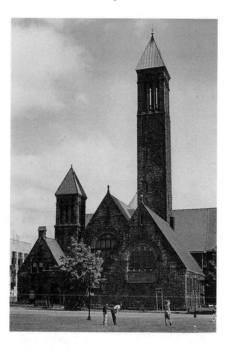

This congregation was organized in 1812, and is the oldest congregation in Buffalo. The Romanesque exterior of the church is Medina sandstone. The vaulted and domed interior with a Greek Cross floor plan has elaborate mosaic pictures and decorations. There are stained glass windows by both Frederick Wilson and Louis Comfort Tiffany. The Jerusalem window is of particular interest. The church tower is derivative from that of St. Philbert's in Tournus, France.

1891 Architects: Green and Wicks

From Wadsworth Street turn left on Arlington Place.

Arlington Park

This square of small charming houses around a common green retains a special feeling of old Buffalo dating to the 1860s. There are various housing styles including a fanciful Gothic Revival at Number 60.

Drive straight ahead and turn right on College Street to Allen Street, left on Allen Street to Delaware Avenue, right on Delaware Avenue and proceed south to Niagara Square. In the center stands the McKinley Monument, which was erected in 1907. This square was originally planned by Joseph Ellicott to be the hub of the downtown area. However, some of the original avenues radiating from this center have now been blocked by other buildings. On the right side of the square is the city hall. If you can park near the square, you may want to tour the next site.

City Hall

65 Niagara Square

This is one of the largest and most outstanding art deco buildings in the country. Built at a cost of nearly seven million dollars, its thirty-two floors rise to 375 feet. The art deco decorations are meant to project an image of Buffalo as a great industrial city of working people. Murals and mosaics on walls, ceilings, and floors give a pictorial history of Buffalo from the Iroquois tribes to the settling and building of the city, the Erie Canal, and the industrial growth of the nineteenth century.

On the thirteenth floor is the Common Council chamber. Its beautiful walnut woodwork is crowned by a superb sunburst skylight ceiling and window artistry meant to be representative of Native American art. The observation tower on the twenty-eighth floor is usually open on weekdays, and affords a wonderful view of the city, Lake Erie, and the Peace Bridge to Canada.

1928 Architects: Wade, Dietel, and Jones

Proceed across the Square and out Delaware Avenue; turn left on Church Street. On the left is the next site.

Old County Hall

92 Franklin Street at Church Street

This Gothic Revival building is dominated by a heavy central clock tower with corner statues of Justice, Commerce, Agriculture, and Mechanical Arts. The interior of the building has been extensively remodeled, although the registry of deed room with its tall cast-iron columns covered with incised ornamentation remains unchanged.

Old County Hall stands on the site of Buffalo's first cemetery. In 1813 the village of Buffalo was surrendered to the British who subsequently burned it to the ground. The small park in front of the building was designed by Frederick Law Olmsted to create a visual base for the structure similar to his design for the Capitol in Washington, D.C.

1876 Architect: A. J. Walker

Now on the right on Church Street at Pearl Street you will see the next two sites. Park or stop if it is possible.

Guaranty Building

28 Church Street at Pearl Street

This thirteen-story structure is considered one of Louis Sullivan's most beautiful skyscrapers. The steel-framed office building was built for and by the Guaranty Construction Company in 1896. Two years later it was sold to the Prudential Insurance Company.

Buffalo almost lost this building to demolition in the early 1980s, but a determined preservation campaign saved it.

The terra cotta facade is intricately decorated with nature motifs.

The lobby has been restored to its original beauty. The restoration uncovered the elaborate iron grilles enclosing the elevators, the wall mosaics, and the unique and lovely stained glass skylight. The iron stairway is of particular interest.

The building is a national historic landmark.

1896 Architects: Adler and Sullivan
1981 Restoration: Cannon Design

St. Paul's Episcopal Cathedral

Church Street at Pearl Street

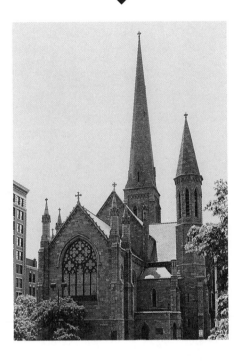

St. Paul's was incorporated in February 1817. This Gothic Revival church was almost destroyed by fire in May 1888. During its rebuilding, services were held at Temple Beth Zion. The church is 175 feet by 94 feet. The bell tower rises 274 feet, and the fourteen bells play several times each day. The church contains many historic memorials, lovely stained glass windows, a hammer-beam roof, and a five-thousand-pipe organ. The Oratory Altar contains a fourteenth-century painting by Jan Pollack. The cathedral is a gathering place for the central business district. Its concerts and other musical offerings are a year-round drawing card to the Western New York community. Concerts at noon on Fridays are especially well-known.

The church is designated a national historic landmark.

1851 Architect: Richard Upjohn

Proceed on Church Street, which will become South Division Street; next building to view will be on the right at the corner of Main Street.

Ellicott Square Building

295 Main Street

This office building was constructed around a central glass-covered court, and in the year it was built was the largest commercial office building in the world. With its decorative stairways and elevators, the atrium is one of the most ornamental public spaces in Buffalo. The elaborate floor mosaics in the atrium were done by W. W. Kent in 1931. This building was placed on land originally set aside for the founder of Buffalo, Joseph Ellicott.

1896 Architects: Daniel H. Burnham and Company

Proceed on South Division Street to the next building at the corner of Ellicott Street.

Erie Community College City Campus

121 Ellicott Street

This structure was built by the United States government for a post office, federal courts, and other government offices, and was renovated in 1981 for the City Campus of Erie Community College. It is built around a sky-lighted central court with four floors of open galleries. The original ornate mosaics remain, and the woodwork in the courtrooms was restored to make classrooms and a law library. The renovations opened the glass ceiling that had covered the first floor of the old building under which mail had been sorted. This allows for a floor view of the galleries from the atrium space that shows off the beauty of this old building in a new way. The college takes great pride in its unique campus.

1901 Architects: O'Rourke, Aiken, Taylor, Metzger, Kent
1981 Adaptive Reuse: Cannon Design

Turn right on Oak Street and proceed across Swan Street and up the ramp to Route 190 North for a view of Buffalo and the waterfront. As you pass Swan Street at the foot of the ramp, look right to the Dun Building and Pilot Field.

Dun Building

110 Pearl Street

As you look up Swan Street, you will see the Dun Building standing alone. This early office building's narrow width demanded bracing from strong winds. The building has an interior steel frame with exterior load-bearing masonry walls. The large arches and the yellow Roman brick cladding are of particular interest.

1895 Architects: Green and Wicks

Pilot Field

From the Route 190 ramp, still looking to the right, you will see one of Buffalo's newest structures, the home field for Buffalo's Triple-A baseball club, the Buffalo Bisons. This is considered a successful effort to retain the turn-of-the-century appearance of this neighborhood while providing a thoroughly modern sports facility.

1988 Architects: Hellmuth, Obata, and Kassabaum

Buffalo Skyline

from Route 190 North

As you circle the skyline, look south to the remaining monumental grain elevators that made Buffalo at one time the largest grain port in the world. Only twelve of what were more than fifty-five elevators remain, but they are still an impressive sight. These elevators were built along the Buffalo River and shipping canals, and their innovative design allowed grain to be loaded directly into ships. Pillsbury Mills, now British owned, is one of several elevators still in operation.

Beyond the elevators you can see the city of Lackawanna and the idled steel mills. This extensive milling area gives a picture of the industrial base of old Buffalo and the source of much of the wealth that financed the buildings you have been viewing.

Continue on Route 190 North.

Buffalo Waterfront

Look to the west over Lake Erie. Buffalo is still a port city with one of the best lake waterfronts in the United States. You can see the Buffalo Lighthouse, which was built in 1833. Its hat-shaped top, called "Chinaman's Light," was a beacon for lake vessels in the last century. Route 190 travels over part of the old Erie Canal, which opened in 1825. With the coming of railway transportation in 1845, Buffalo was placed at the center of a major transportation network. It kept this status for over a hundred years.

Illuminating Gas Company

294 Genesee Street

Looking below to the right (after passing Exit N7), you will see the old Illuminating Gas Company Works. This building was once at the edge of the lake and on the Erie Canal, so that coal could be delivered by ship or barge for the manufacture of illuminating gas. Notice the 250-foot brick facade dressed with ashlar masonry.

1848, 1859, 1877 Architect: John H. Selkirk

Exit Route 190 at Exit N8, Niagara Street–South. Turn right on Niagara Street, left on West Huron Street to Delaware Avenue, and left on Delaware Avenue. You will now proceed north on Delaware Avenue for 3.1 miles.

The Midway

471–499 Delaware Avenue

Driving north on Delaware Avenue between Niagara Square and Forest Lawn Cemetery you will see a special group of houses built at the turn of the century. Row houses of this elegance and neoclassical style are unusual in Buffalo. Each house was built by an individual owner, usually a business or professional person. It is called "The Midway" because the houses are located half the distance between the square and Forest Lawn.

1889–95   Architects: Green and
                        Wicks;
                        Marling and
                        Johnson

Wilcox House

631 Delaware Avenue

It was in this house that Theodore Roosevelt was sworn in as president of the United States in September 1901, after the assassination in Buffalo of President William McKinley, who was visiting the Pan-American Exposition. The oldest part of the house was originally a brick barracks and did not face the avenue. In 1845 it was purchased as a home, and the handsome Greek Revival style portico, as well as a two-story wing in the back was added to the Delaware Avenue side. In the 1890s, a morning room and a dining room were designed. The house is now operated by the Department of the Interior as the Theodore Roosevelt National Historic Site. The house is open to the public.

Proceed north along Delaware Avenue to Gates Circle. Follow Delaware Avenue out of Gates Circle (this is the second right out of the Circle). Forest Lawn Cemetery will be on your right at Delavan Avenue.

Forest Lawn Cemetery

entrance at Delavan Avenue

This large cemetery was incorporated by Olmsted in his park system for Buffalo. It is in the tradition of beautiful park cemeteries, and it includes curving drives, rolling vistas, a reflection pool, and intriguing monuments. The cemetery is surrounded by a handsome iron fence, and over the years it has become a bird sanctuary and a favorite walking place for Buffalonians.

A guidebook is available at the gatehouse for detailed walking and driving tours, history of the cemetery, and well-known individuals who are buried there.

After you pass the cemetery, on your left you will be able to view Delaware Park Lake.

From Delaware Avenue take Exit Route 198 East for .6 mile, then take Exit NY 5–Main Street (this exit will be on the right), turn left on Main Street and return to the South Campus of the University at Buffalo.

Illustration Credits

◆

All photographs in this book were taken by Gwen A. Howard, with the exception of the following:

Cary–Farber–Sherman Halls, Dorsheimer Lab/Greenhouse, Lockwood Memorial Library, and Squire Hall (photographs courtesy of University at Buffalo Office of Publications)

Abbott Hall, Acheson Hall, Crosby Hall, and Diefendorf Hall (photographs courtesy of the University Archives, State University of New York at Buffalo)

O'Brian Hall, Fine Arts Center, Lake LaSalle, Student Union, Engineering Quadrangle, Wende Hall, Townsend and Beck Halls, Mackay Heating Plant, Clark Hall, Dormitory Quadrangle, Clement Hall, 800 West Ferry Street, Old County Hall, Guaranty Building, St. Paul's Episcopal Cathedral, Ellicott Square Building, Buffalo Skyline, and Buffalo Lighthouse (photographs by George M. Rupley)

Darwin D. Martin House and Gardener's Cottage (photographs by Annegret Richards)

Buffalo Waterfront (photograph copyrighted by Joe Traver)

Area map of the North and South Campuses (courtesy of University of Buffalo Office of Publications)

North and South Campus walking tour maps (designed by Michael Sraga)

Driving tour map (designed by Kay Lohnes and Louise Mink)

Index of Buildings and Sites

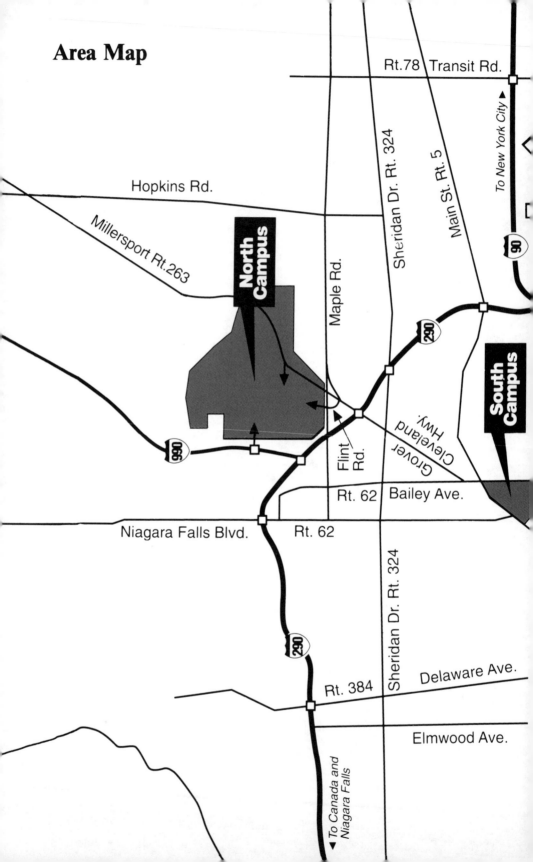

Area Map

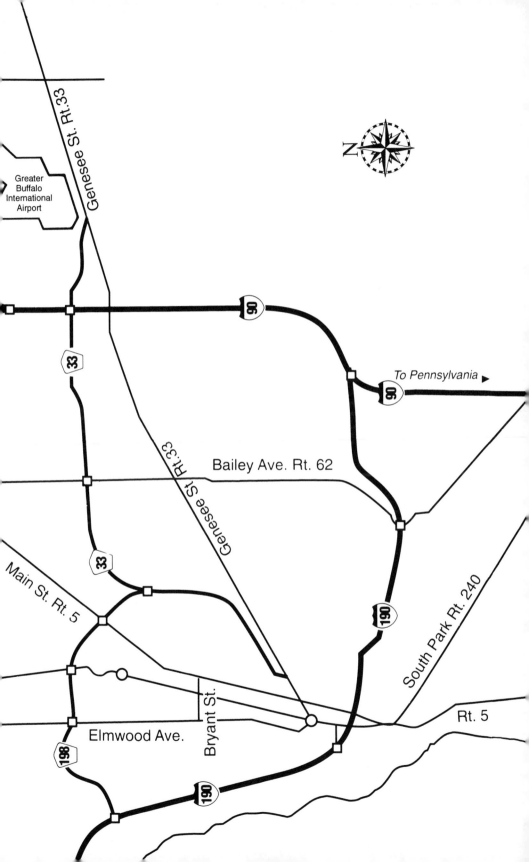